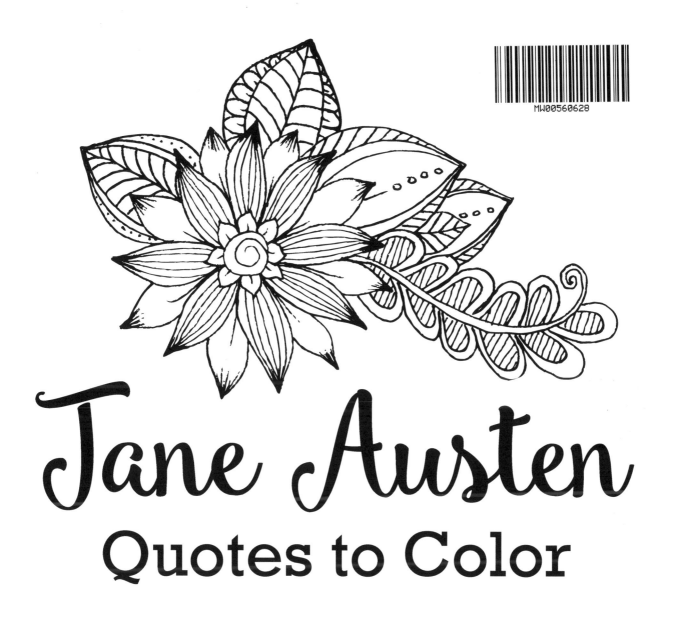

Jane Austen
Quotes to Color

Coloring Quotes
Adult Coloring Book

xist Publishing

Want to hear about more coloring quotes books?

Visit xistpublishing.com/color

to sign up for our Coloring Quotes newsletter and get a free
exclusive printable coloring page.

Quotes from Jane Austen
Designed by Calee M. Lee
with images from Fotolia
Design Copyright © 2016 Calee M. Lee
ISBN: 978-1-5324-0005-6
Published by Xist Publishing in 2016
PO Box 61593, Irvine CA 92602
www.xistpublishing.com

You must allow me to tell you how ardently I

admire and love you

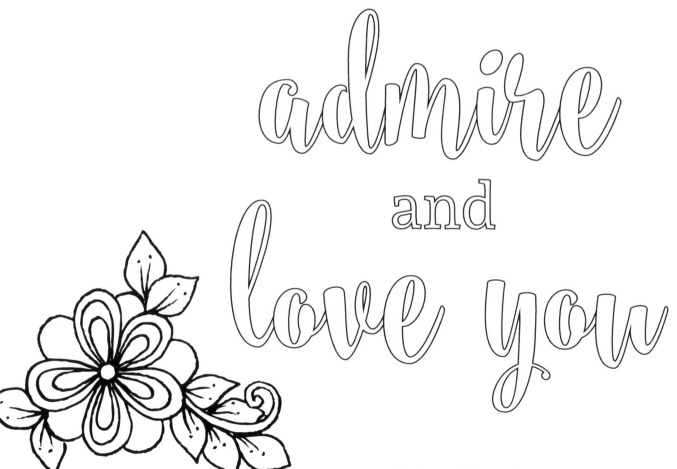

Pride and Prejudice

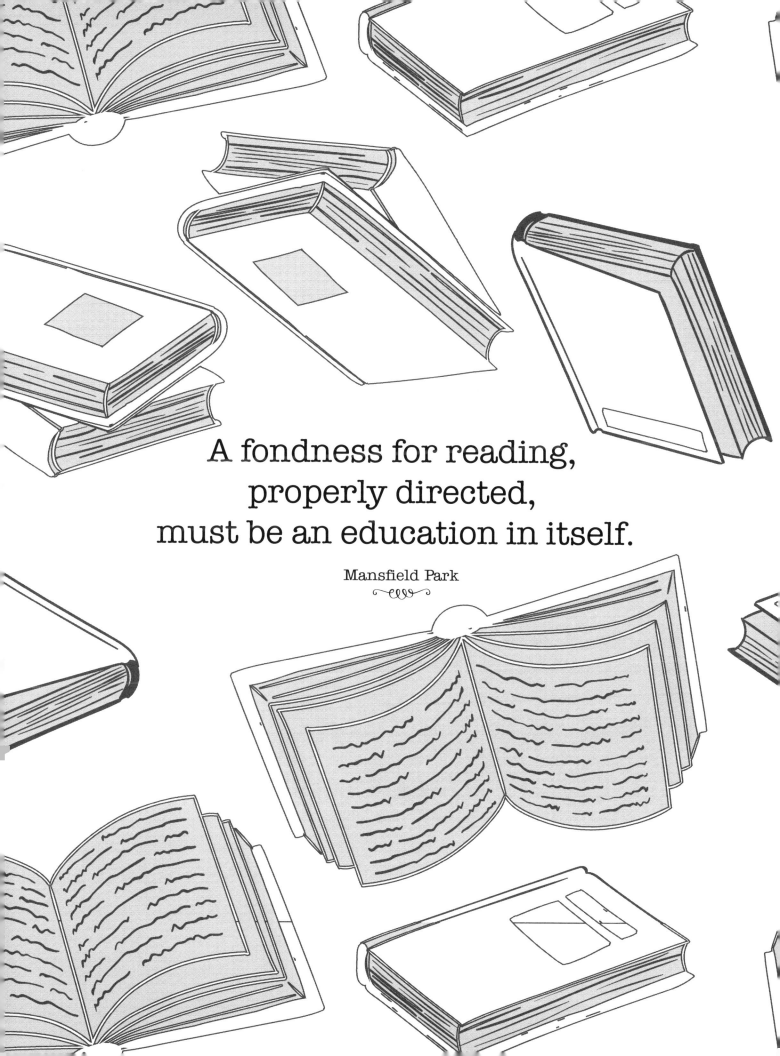

A fondness for reading,
properly directed,
must be an education in itself.

Mansfield Park

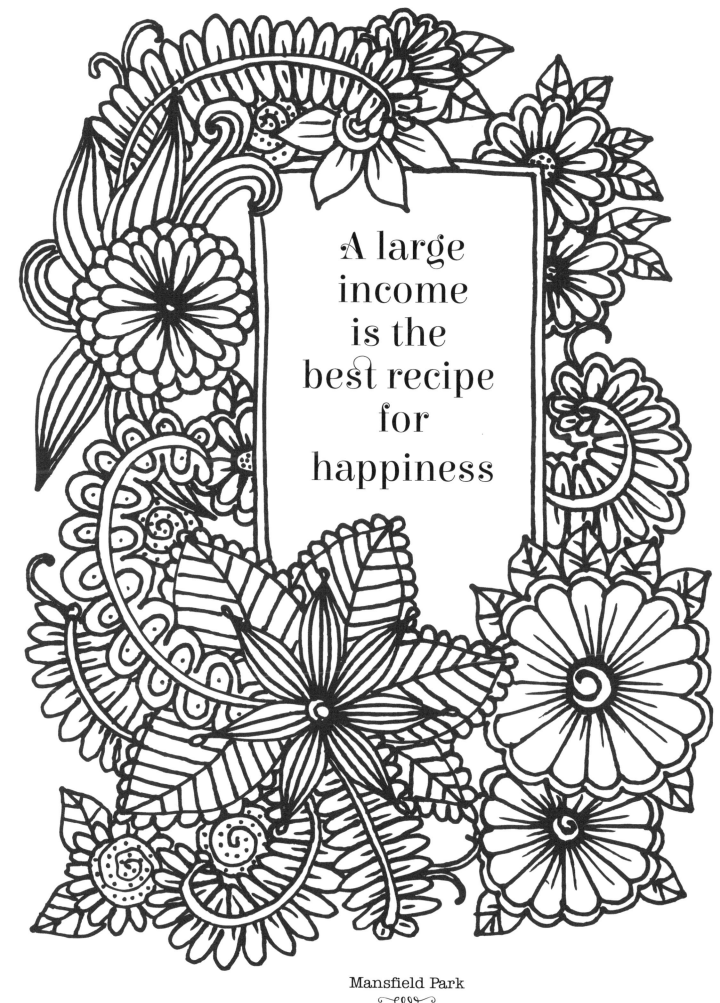

A large
income
is the
best recipe
for
happiness

Mansfield Park

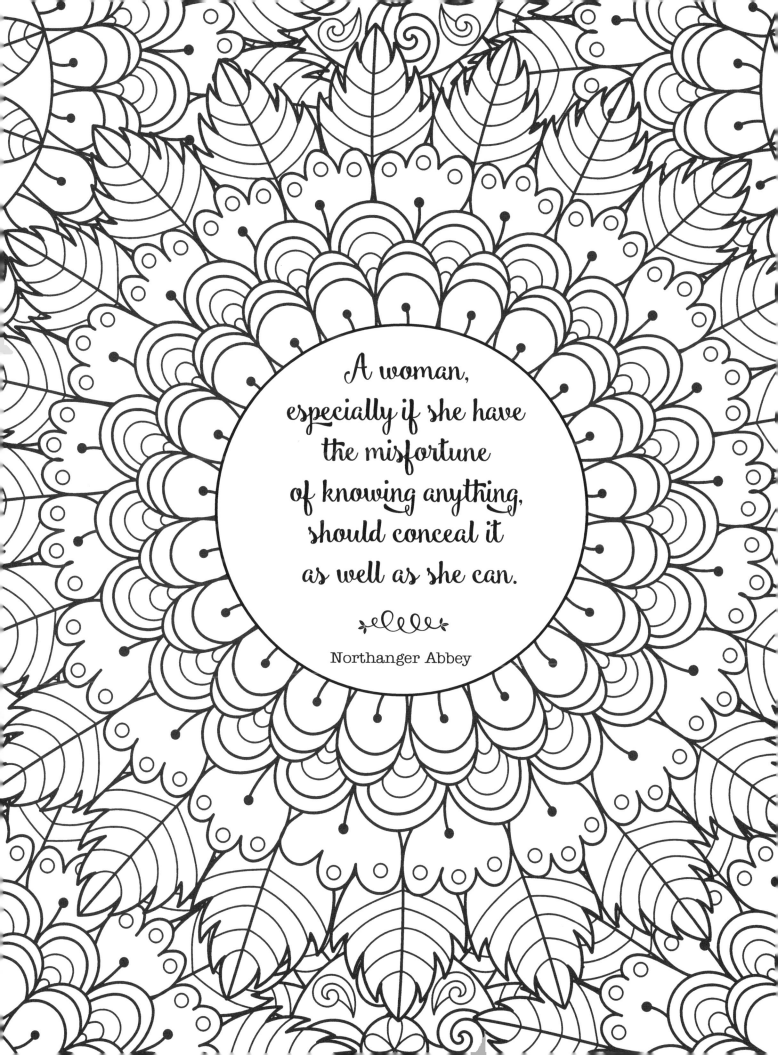

A woman,
especially if she have
the misfortune
of knowing anything,
should conceal it
as well as she can.

Northanger Abbey

One cannot have too large a

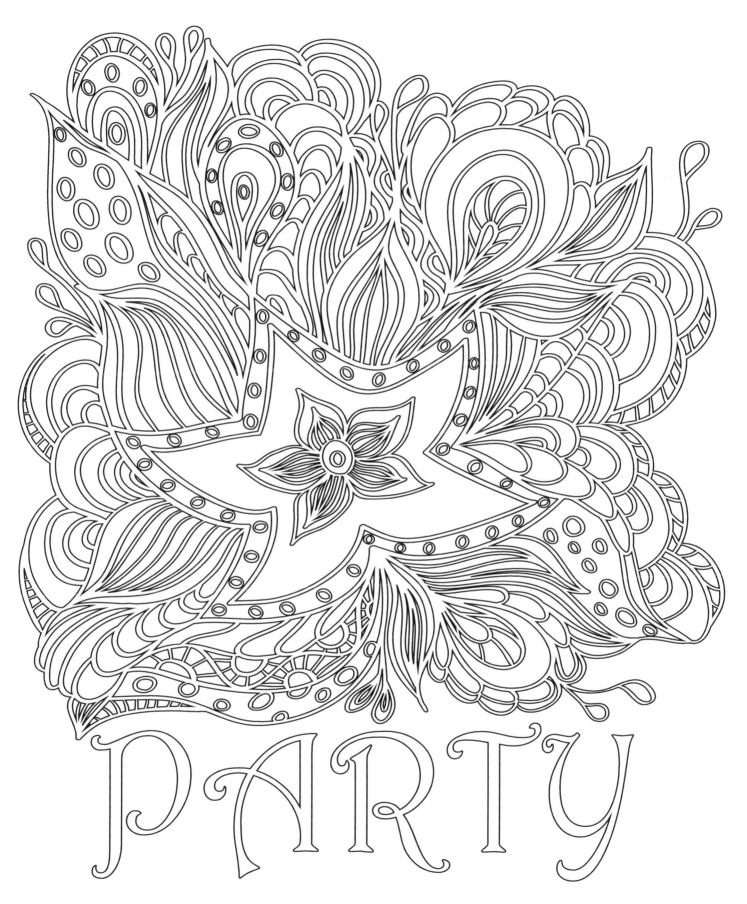

PARTY

Emma

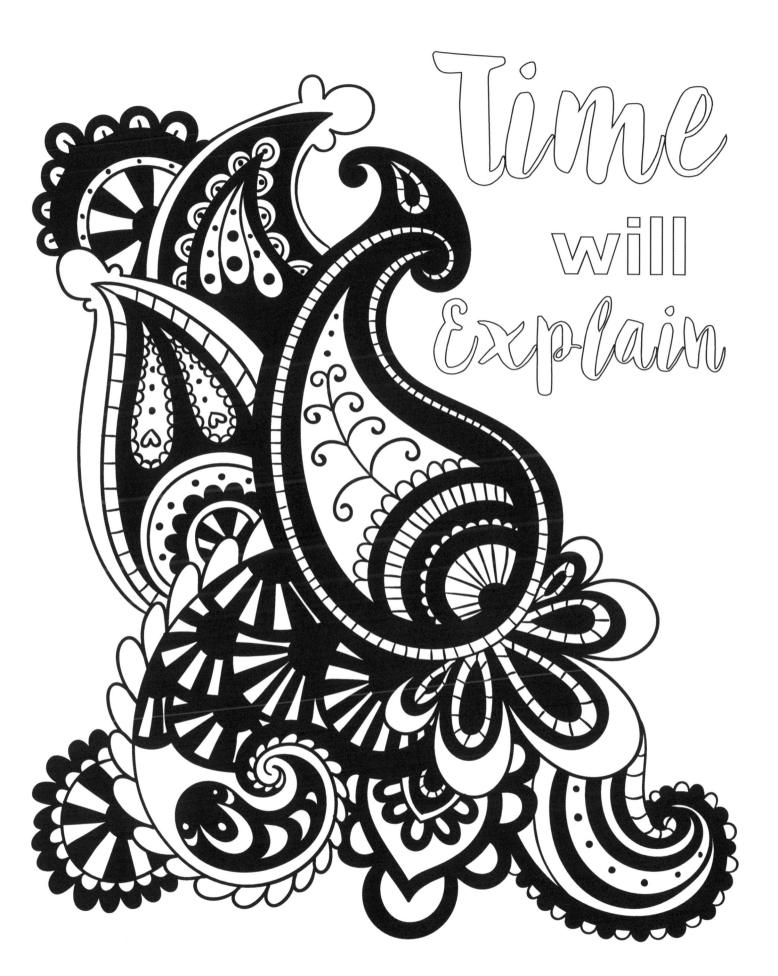

Time will Explain

Persuasion

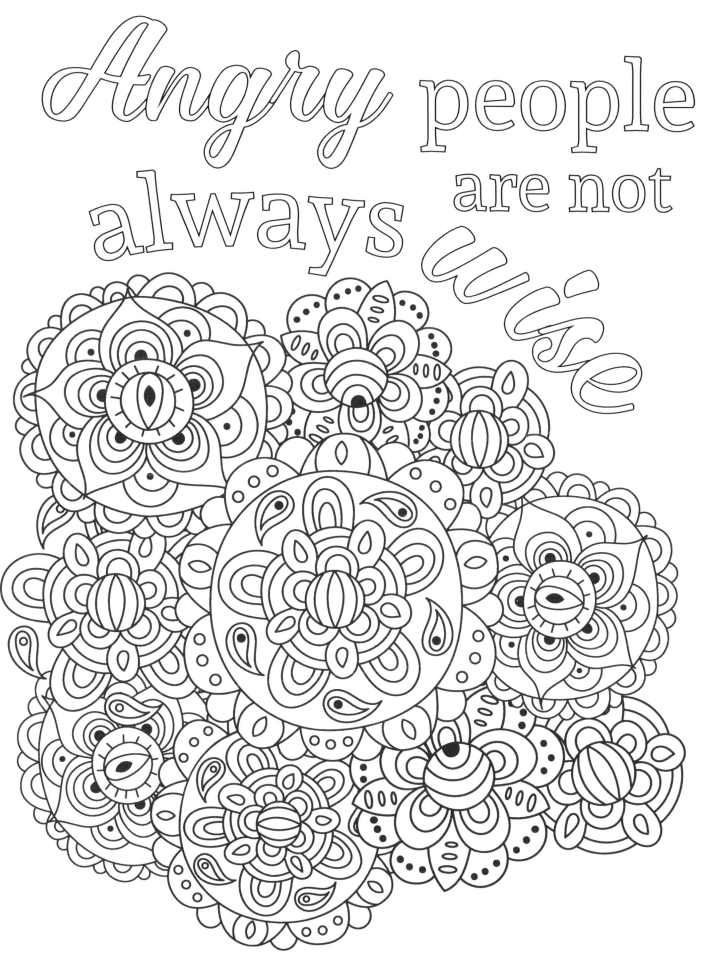

Angry people are not always wise

Pride and Prejudice

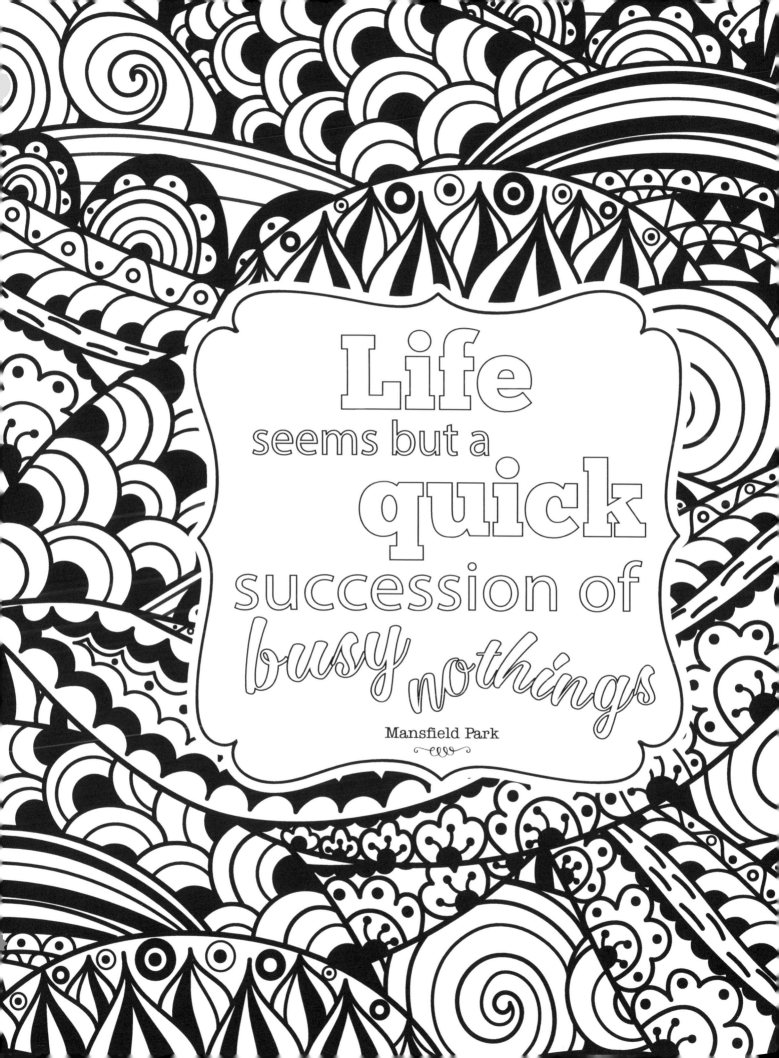

Life
seems but a
quick
succession of
busy nothings

Mansfield Park

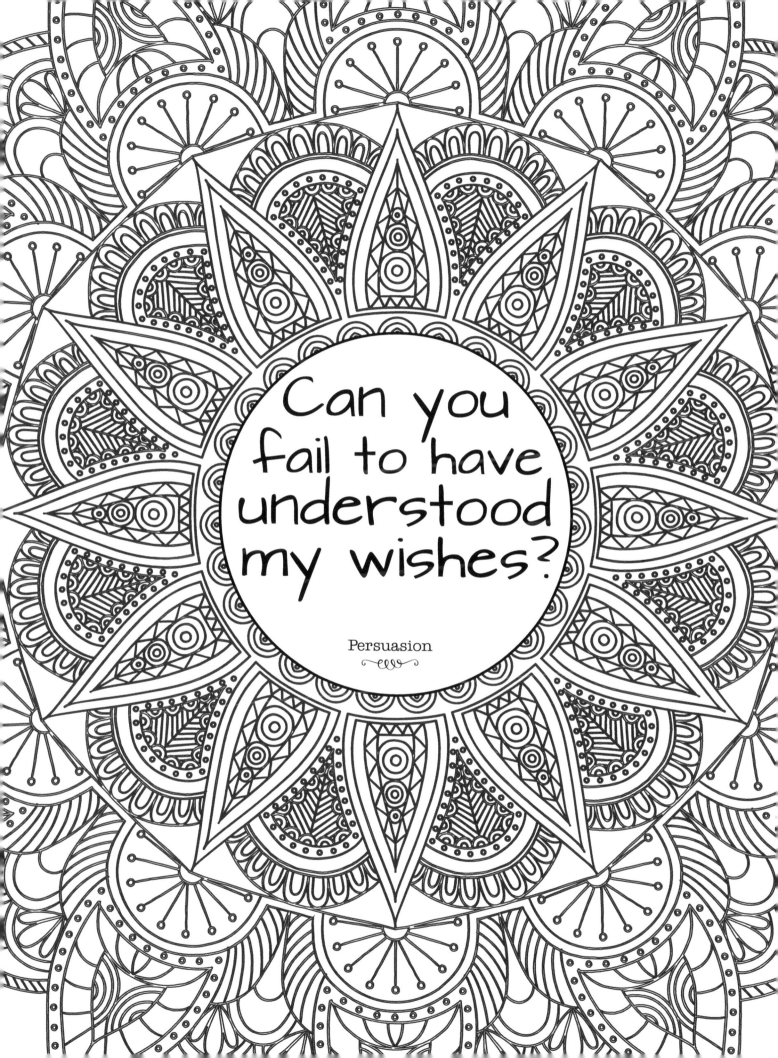

Can you fail to have understood my wishes?

Persuasion

I HAVE FAULTS ENOUGH

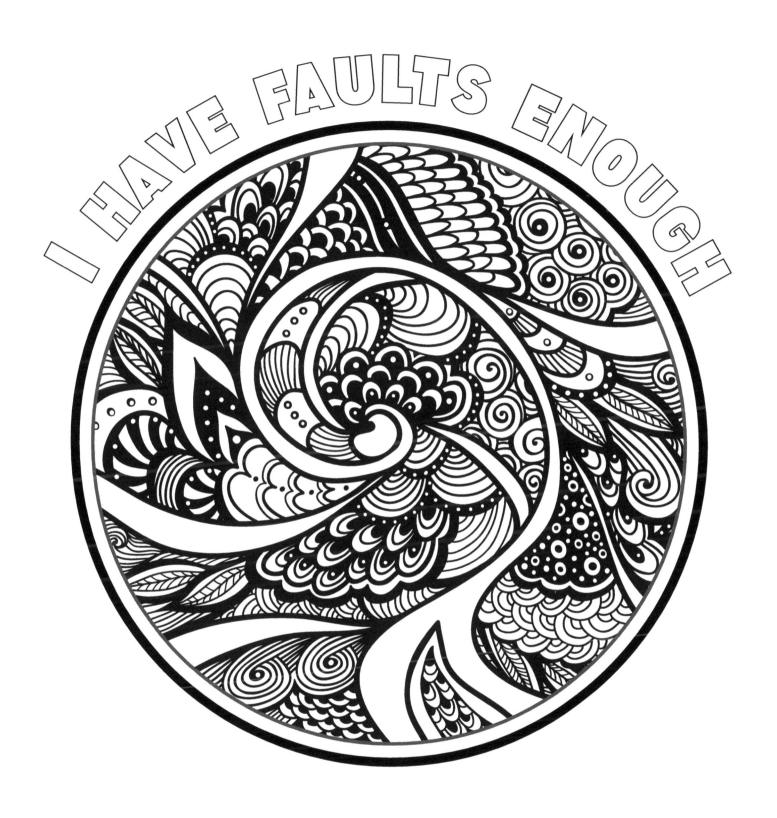

Pride and Prejudice

We do not

SUFFER

by

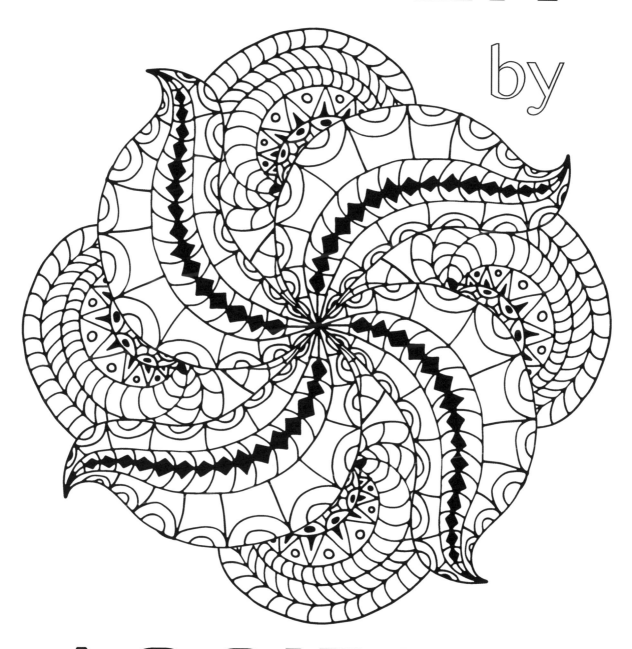

ACCIDENT

Northanger Abbey

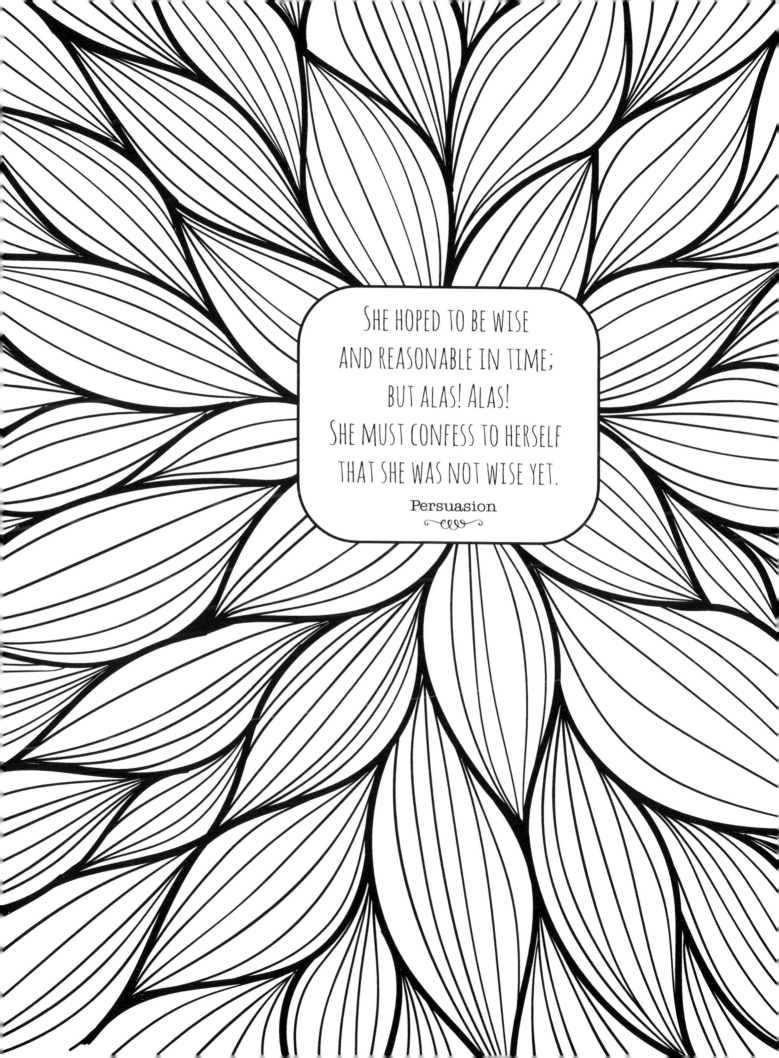

She hoped to be wise
and reasonable in time;
but alas! Alas!
She must confess to herself
that she was not wise yet.

Persuasion

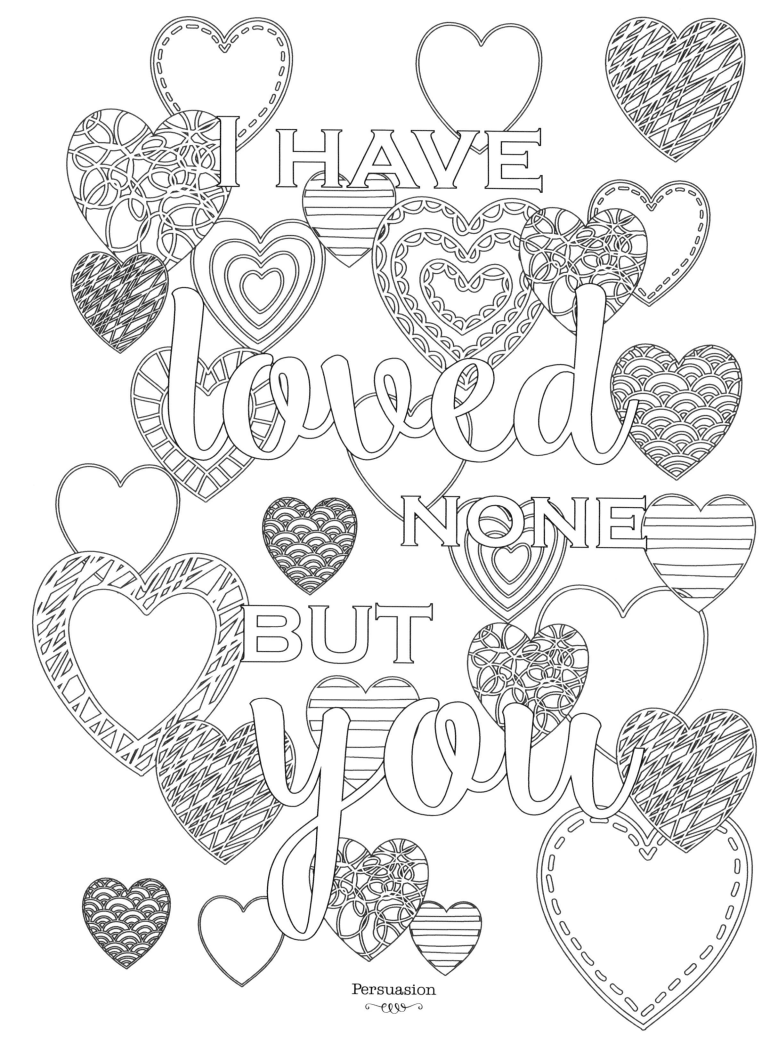

I HAVE loved NONE BUT you

Persuasion

IN VAIN I HAVE STRUGGLED

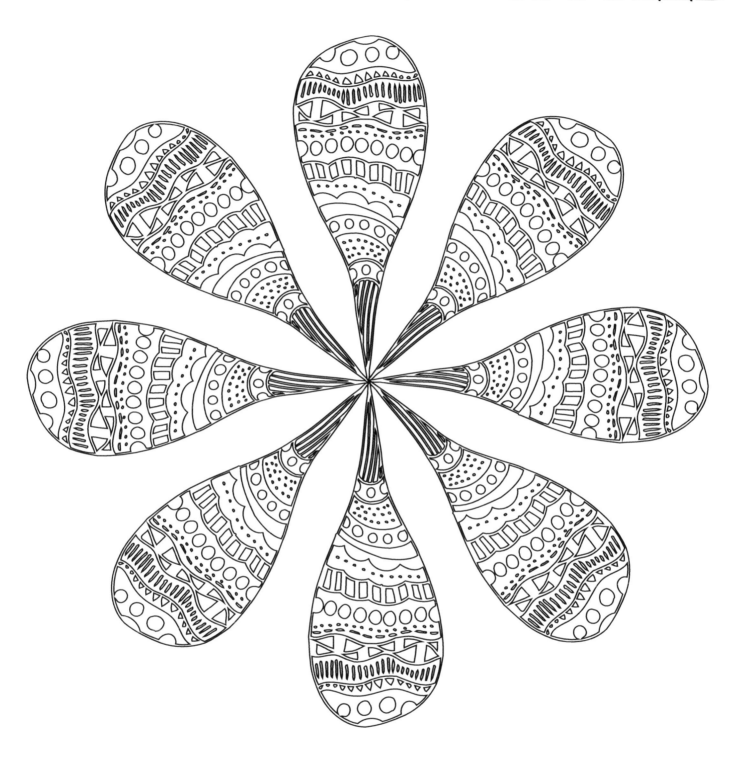

IT WILL NOT DO!

Pride and Prejudice

SELFISHNESS

must

always

be

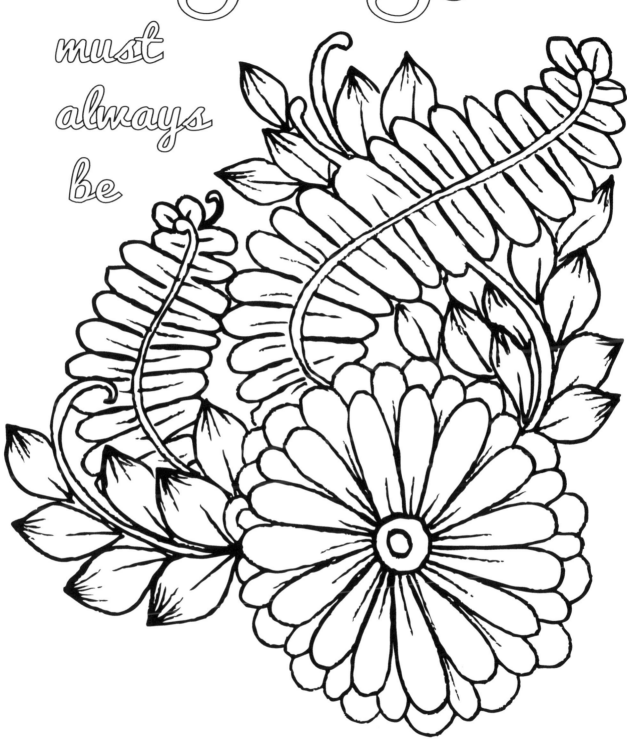

FORGIVEN

Mansfield Park

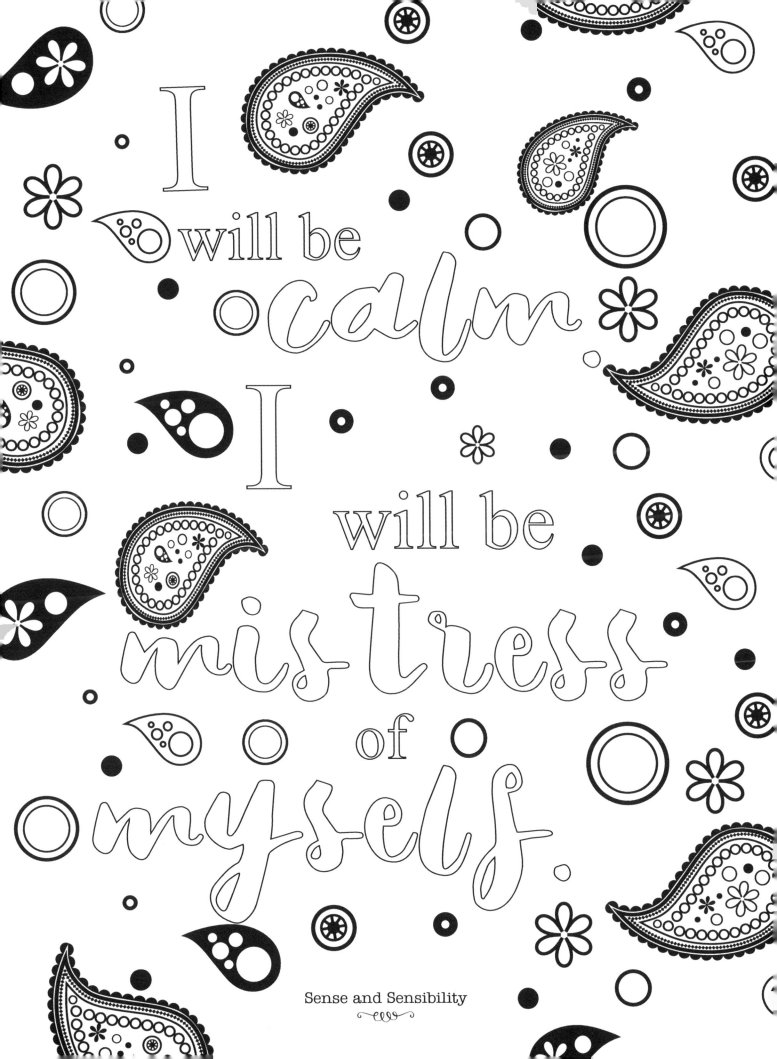

I will be calm. I will be mistress of myself.

Sense and Sensibility

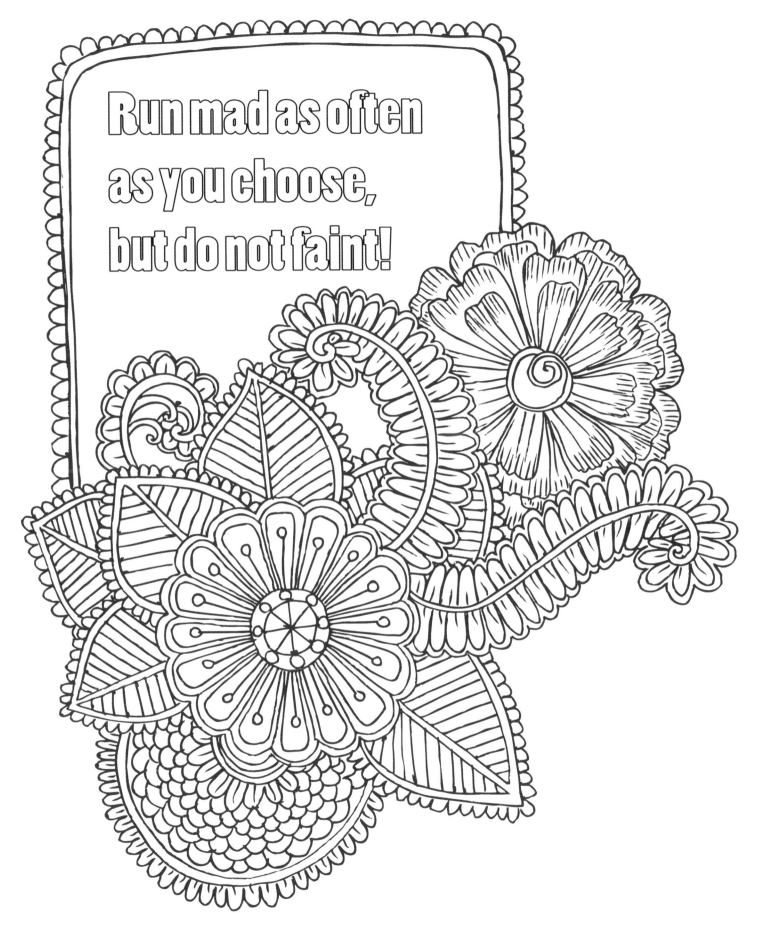

Run mad as often as you choose, but do not faint!

Love and Friendship

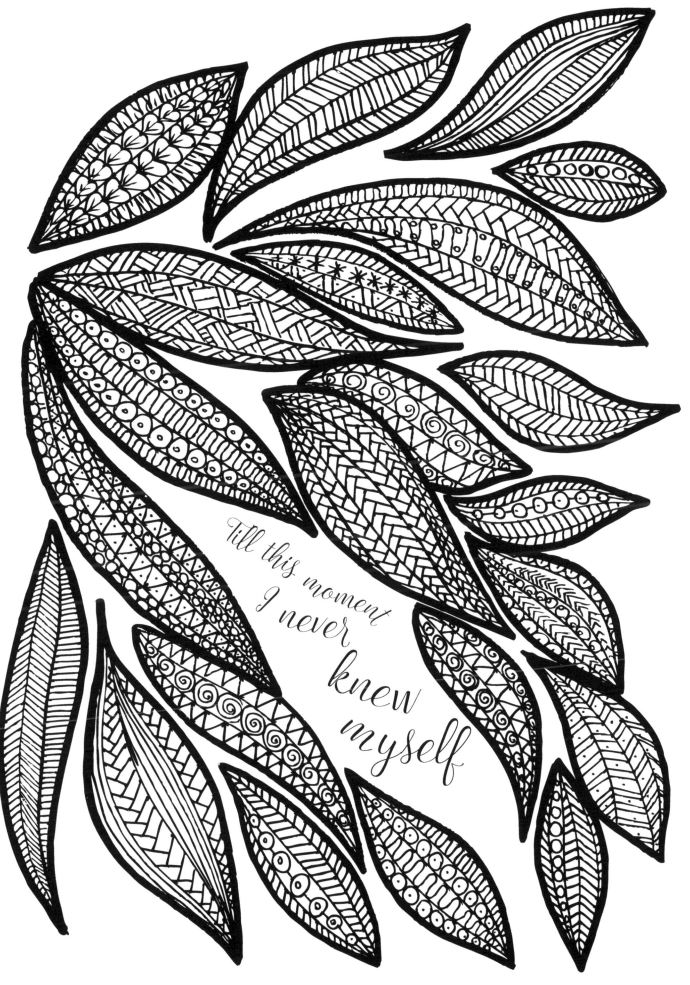

Till this moment I never knew myself

Pride and Prejudice

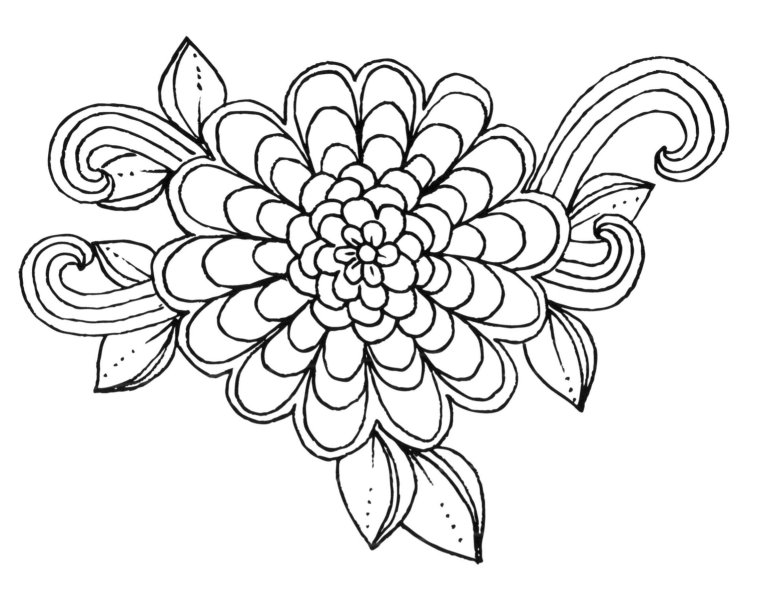

It is very difficult
for the prosperous
to be humble

Emma

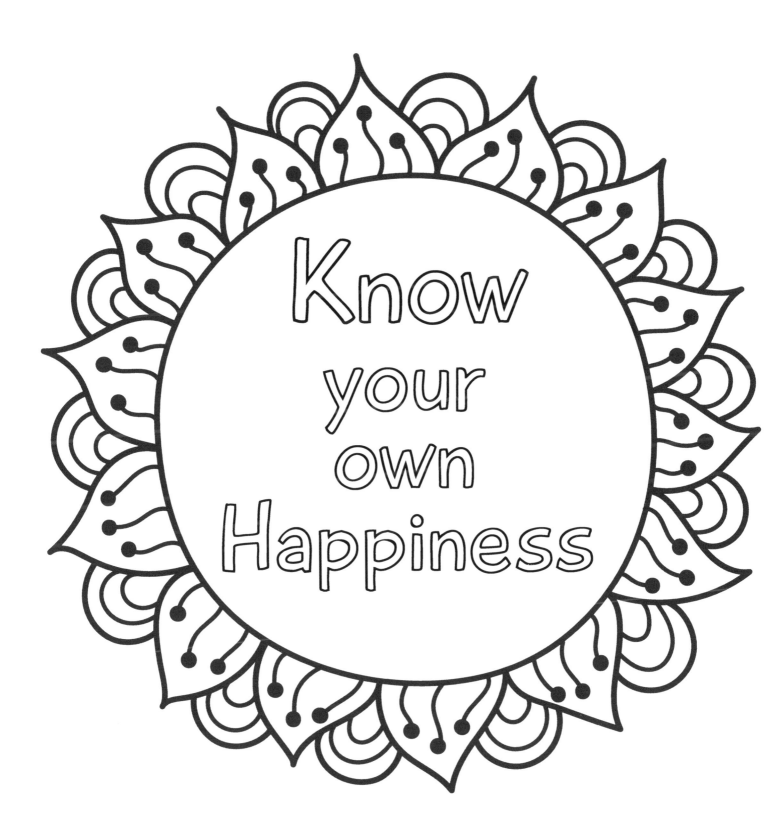

Know your own Happiness

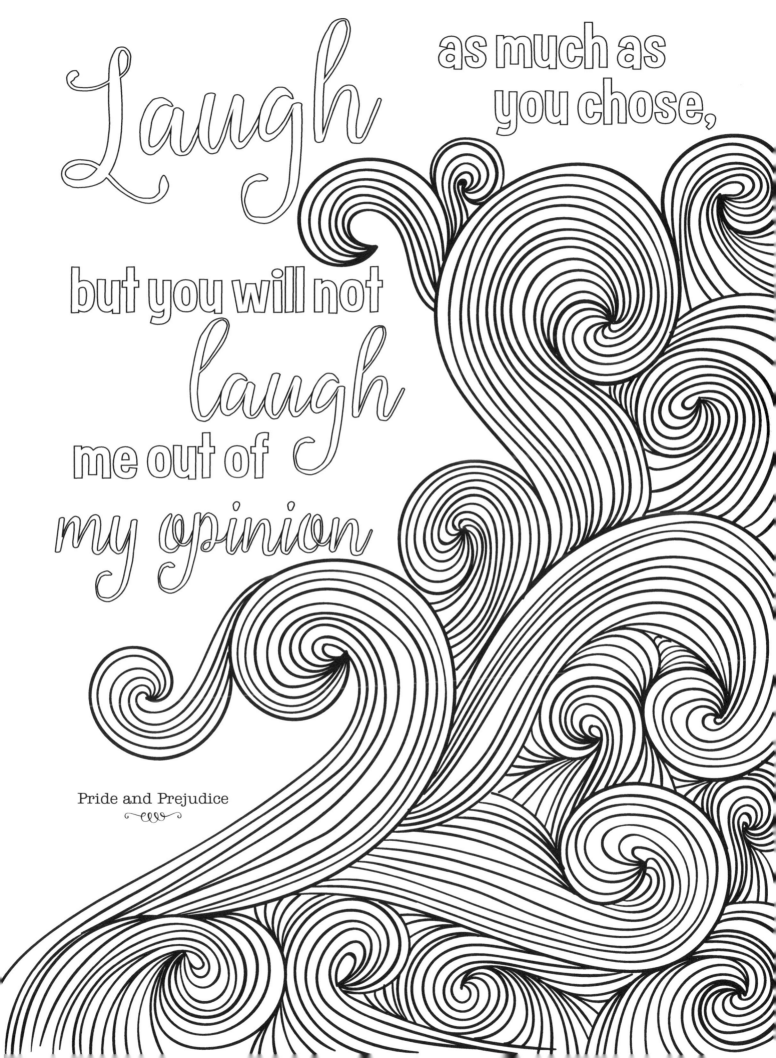

Laugh as much as you chose, but you will not laugh me out of my opinion

Pride and Prejudice

I may have
lost my *heart*

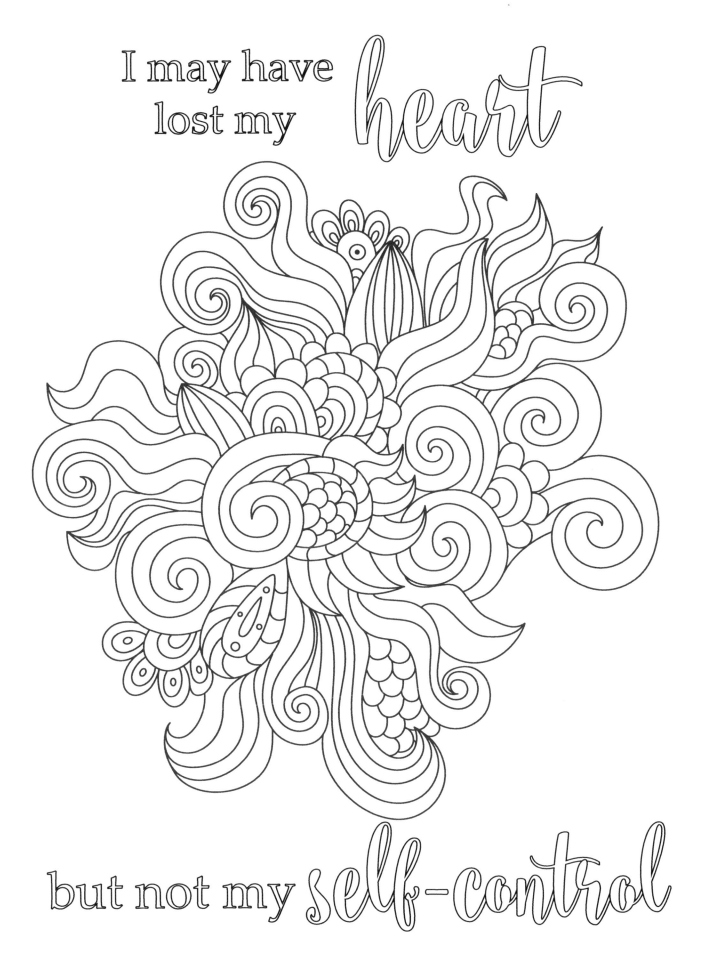

but not my *self-control*

Emma

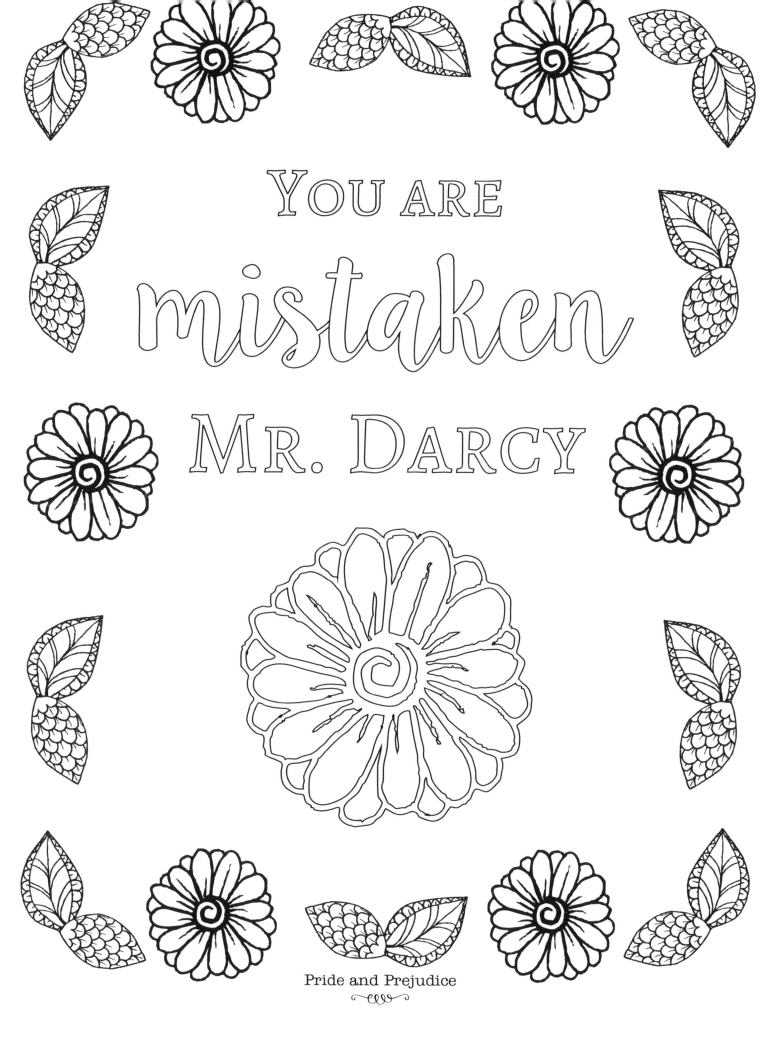

You are mistaken Mr. Darcy

Pride and Prejudice

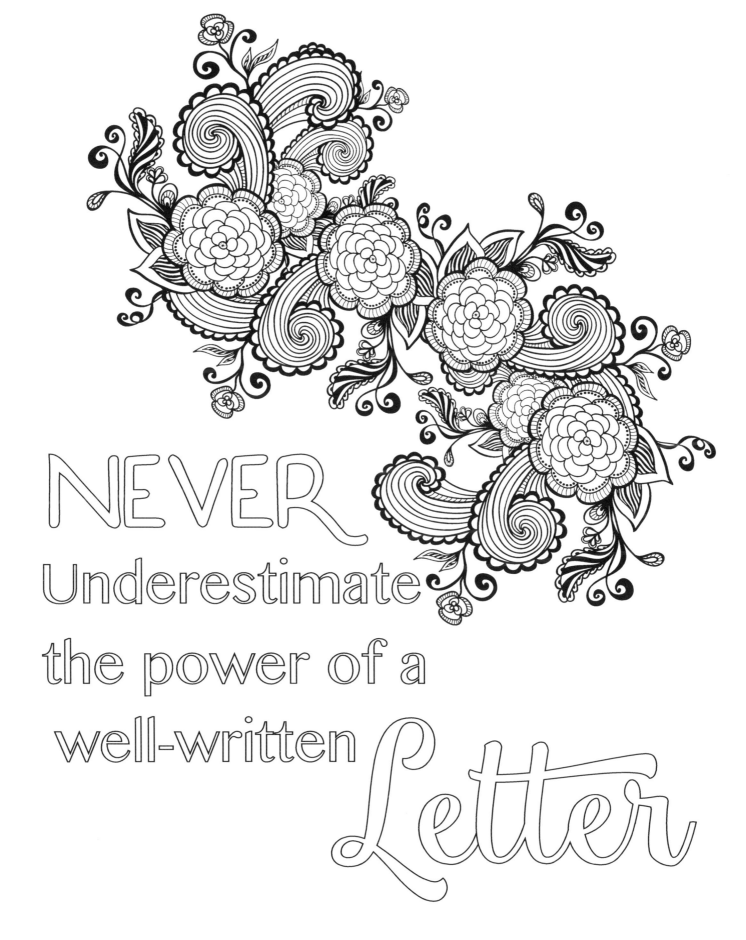

NEVER
Underestimate
the power of a
well-written Letter

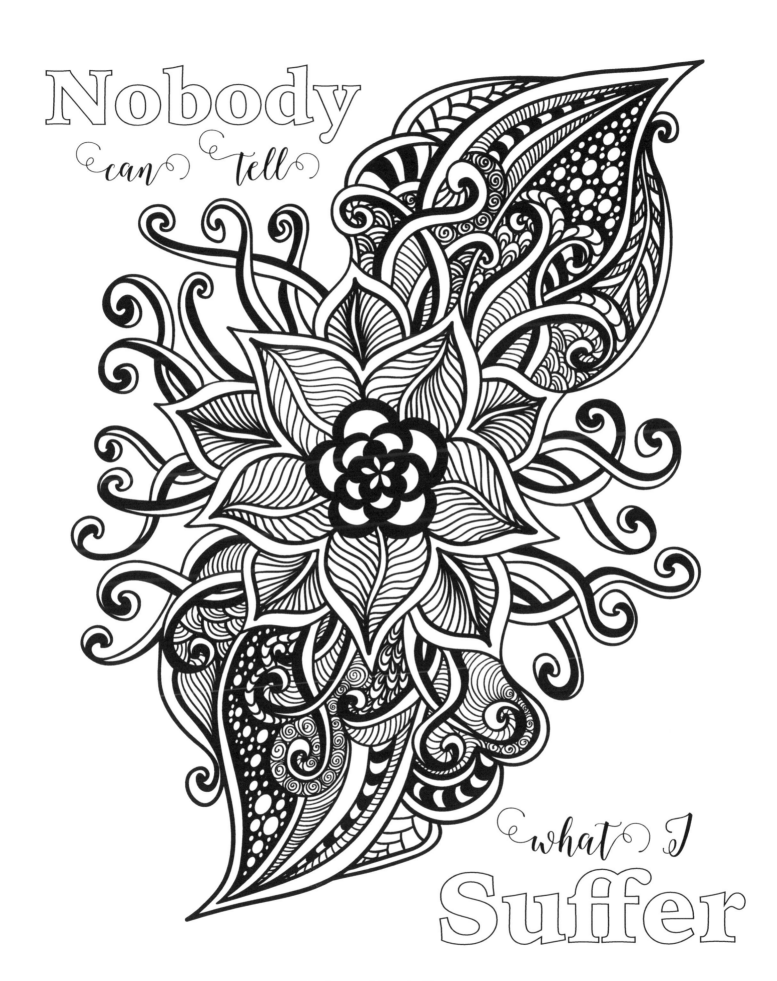

Nobody can tell what I Suffer

Pride and Prejudice

One half of the world

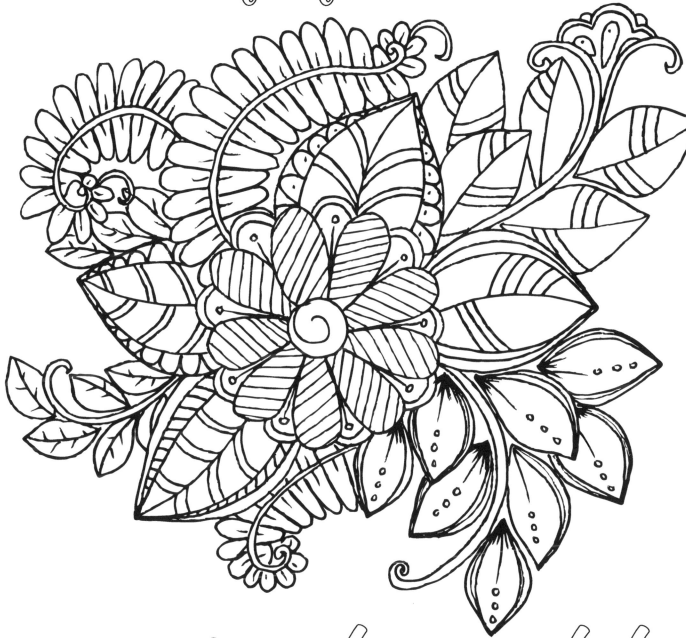

cannot understand the
pleasures of the other

Emma

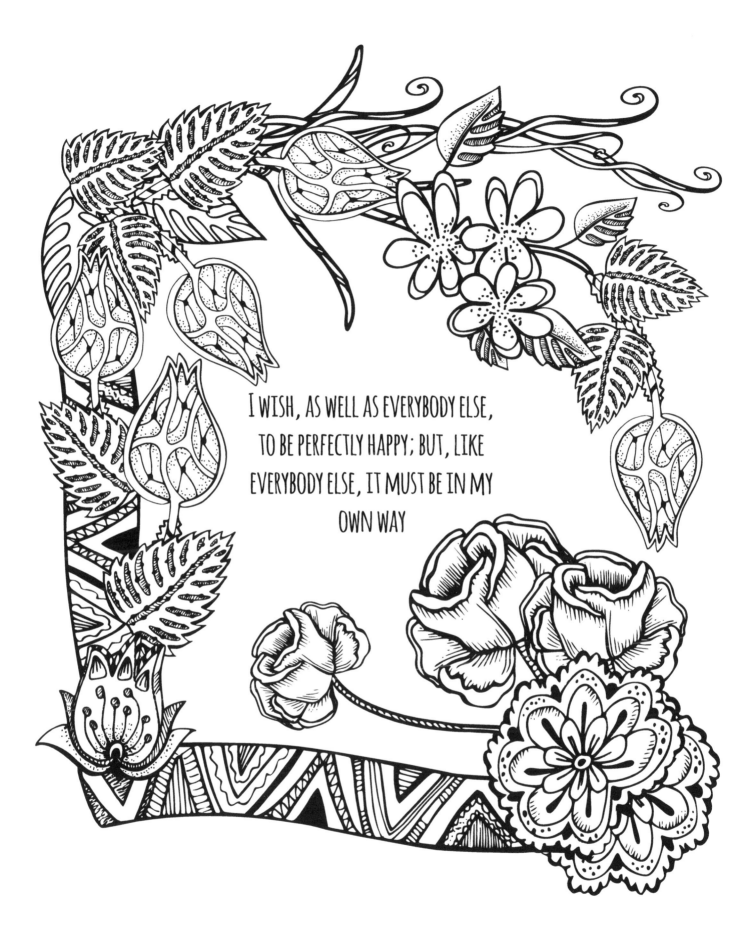

I WISH, AS WELL AS EVERYBODY ELSE, TO BE PERFECTLY HAPPY; BUT, LIKE EVERYBODY ELSE, IT MUST BE IN MY OWN WAY

Sense and Sensibility

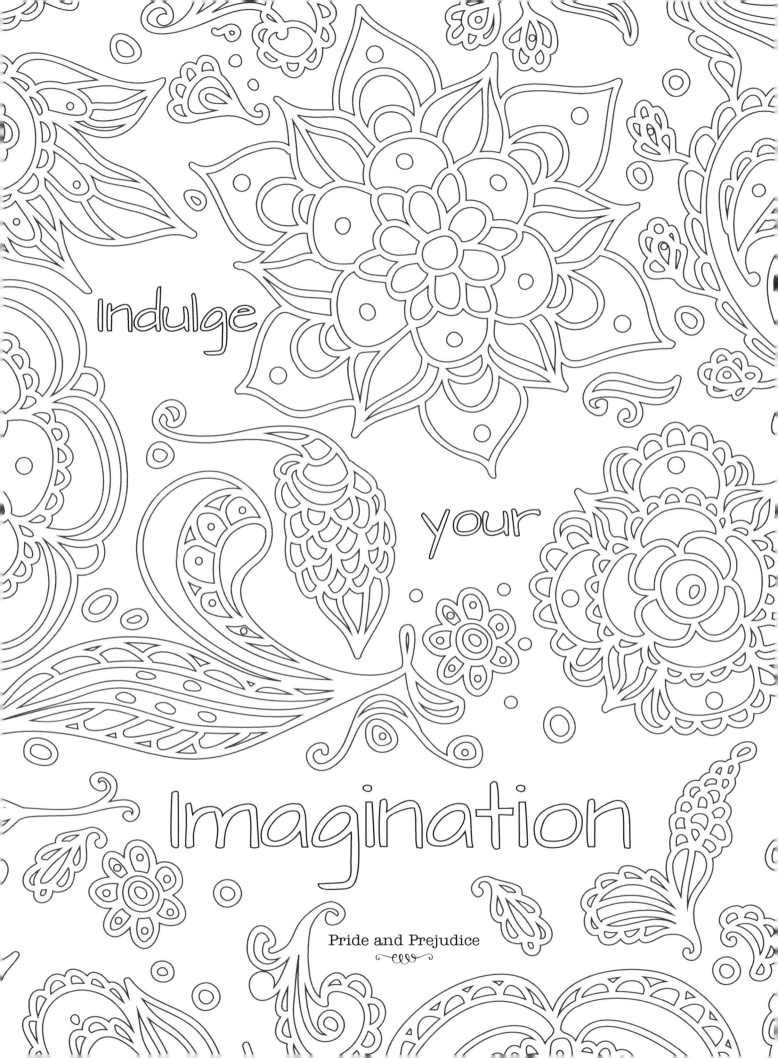

Indulge your Imagination

Pride and Prejudice

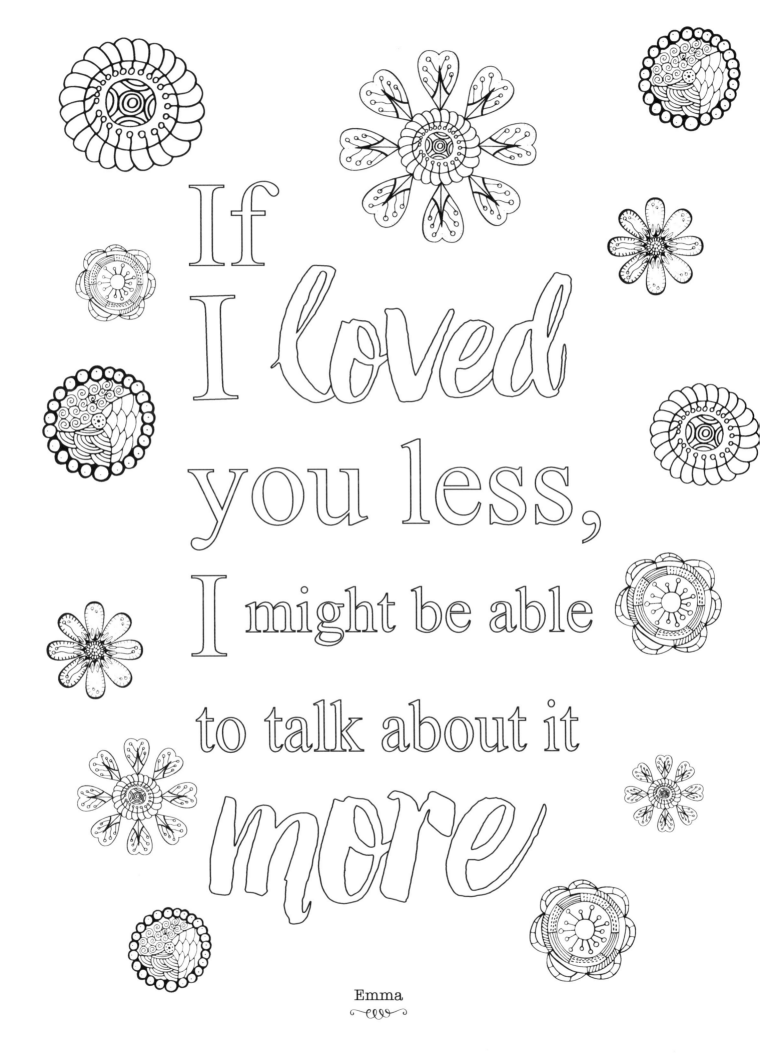

If I *loved* you less, I might be able to talk about it *more*

Emma

There is
I would not do
for my nothing
friends

Northanger Abbey

77935359R00035

Made in the USA
San Bernardino, CA
30 May 2018